1, 2, 3
Count What You See

Julia A. Royston

BK Royston Publishing LLC
P. O. Box 4321
Jeffersonville, IN 47131
http://www.bkroystonpublishing.com
bkroystonpublishing@gmail.com
502.802.5385

Copyright 2022

All Rights Reserved. No part of this book may be reproduced, stored in a retrieval system, or transmitted by any means without the written permission of the author.

Cover Design: Elite Covers
Illustrations: Sanghamitra Dasgupta
Additional Illustrations: Licensed via Shutterstock

ISBN-13: 978-1-959543-00-8

Printed in the USA

Dedication

I dedicate this book to every child on the counting to high level math journey.

Acknowledgements

I first acknowledge my divine and earthly teams that are with me every step of the way. I couldn't do all of this without you.

I thank my husband, Brian K. Royston for everything from his love to technical support, encouragement and care.
Love you forever.

To my family, I love you always.

I acknowledge all of the parents, godparents, foster parents, aunts, uncles, administrators, teachers, school counselors, social workers and case workers who will see a need for this book for a child on their math journey and make sure that they get the help that they need. We appreciate all that you do.

To everyone that shall read, share, purchase, refer and recommend this book to any child, adult and/or organization.
Thank you!

Introduction

At this stage of my business and book publishing journey, I produce what I love and what people need. I published a book titled, "Letters on Sight, Letter We Write" in 2021 and was recently asked, "where is the book for helping younger children with their counting and numbers." Well, here it is.

I trust that this will help children everywhere on their Math journey.

Let's go!

1

One

2

Two

3

Three

4

Four

5

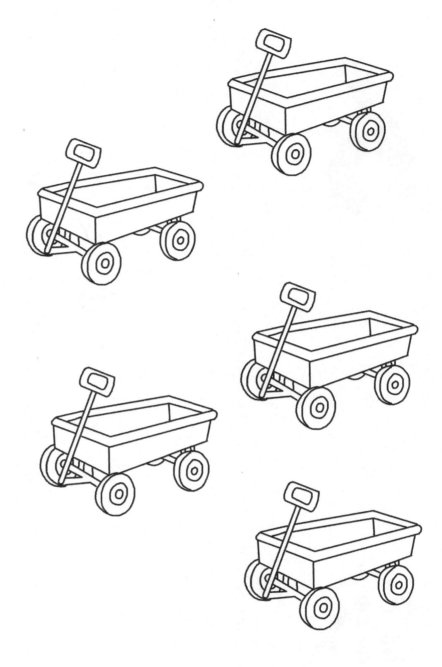

Five

6

Six

7

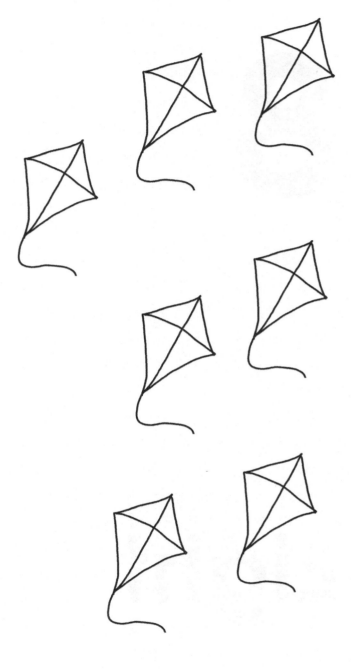

Seven

8

Eight

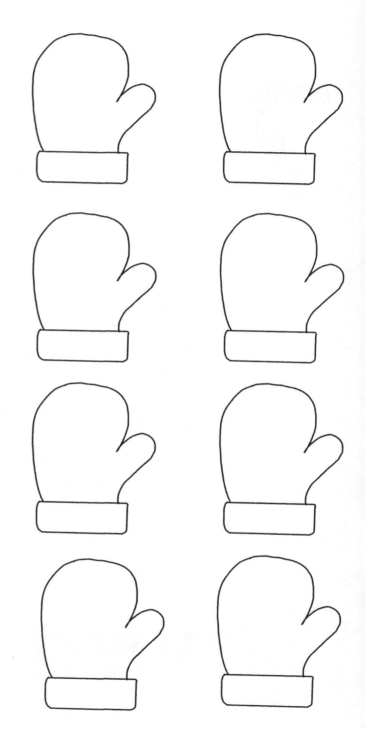

9

Nine

10

Ten

How Many Objects Are on This Page?

_____

How Many Objects Are on This Page?

_____

How Many Objects Are on This Page?

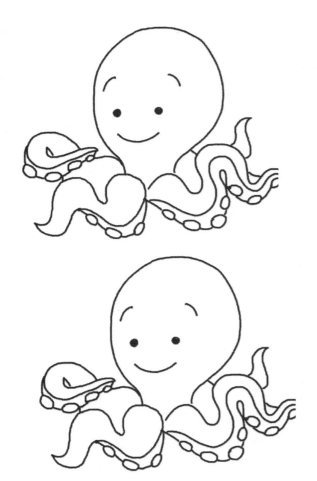

_____

How Many Objects Are on This Page?

_____

How Many Objects Are on This Page?

_____

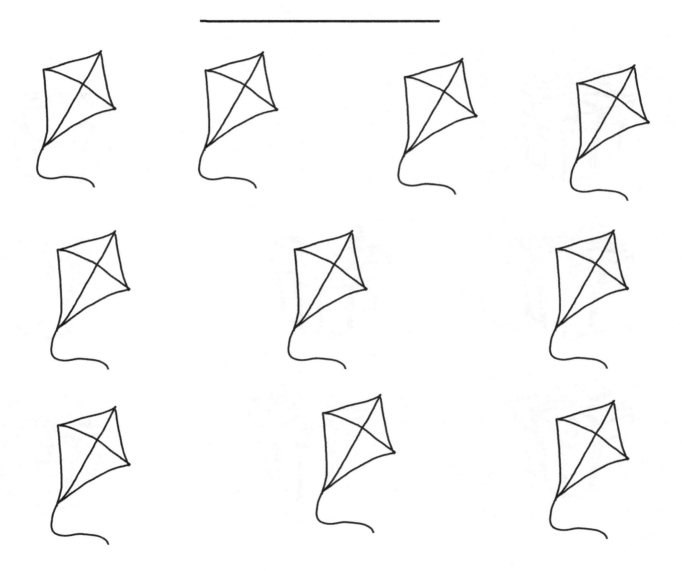

How Many Objects Are on This Page?

_____

Activity #1

Create Your Own Counting Activity. Copy the following pages, cut them out, glue the number of objects on a page and then count them yourself. Put as many objects on a page that will fit and then count them. How many objects did you count?

Let's go!

Activity Page

Paste the amount of objects that you want to count below and then place the number of your objects on the line provided. Let's go! Don't forget to put your name on the paper..

Name:_____

Number of Objects below_____

Activity Page

Paste the amount of objects that you want to count below and then place the number of your objects on the line provided. Let's go! Don't forget to put your name on the paper..

Name:_____

Number of Objects below_____

Activity Page

Paste the amount of objects that you want to count below and then place the number of your objects on the line provided. Let's go! Don't forget to put your name on the paper..

Name:_____

Number of Objects below_____

Activity Page

Paste the amount of objects that you want to count below and then place the number of your objects on the line provided. Let's go! Don't forget to put your name on the paper..

Name:_____

Number of Objects below_____

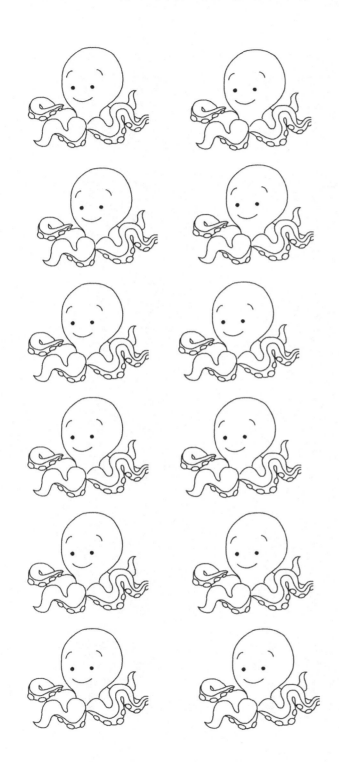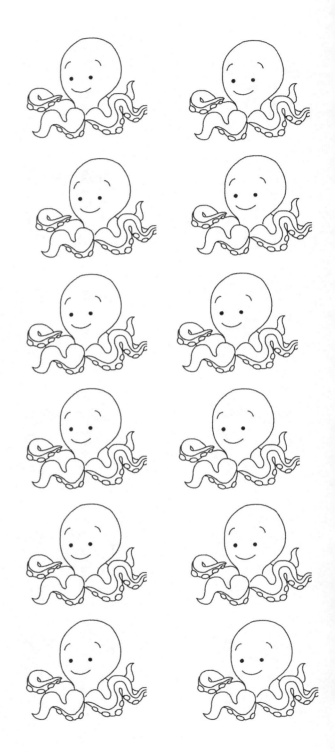

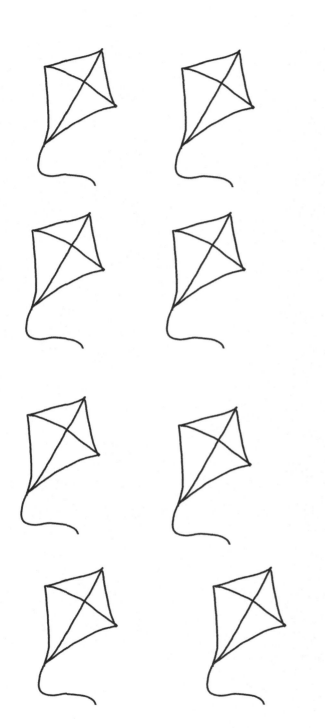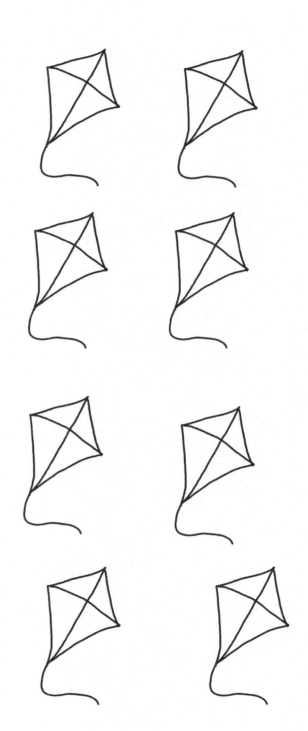

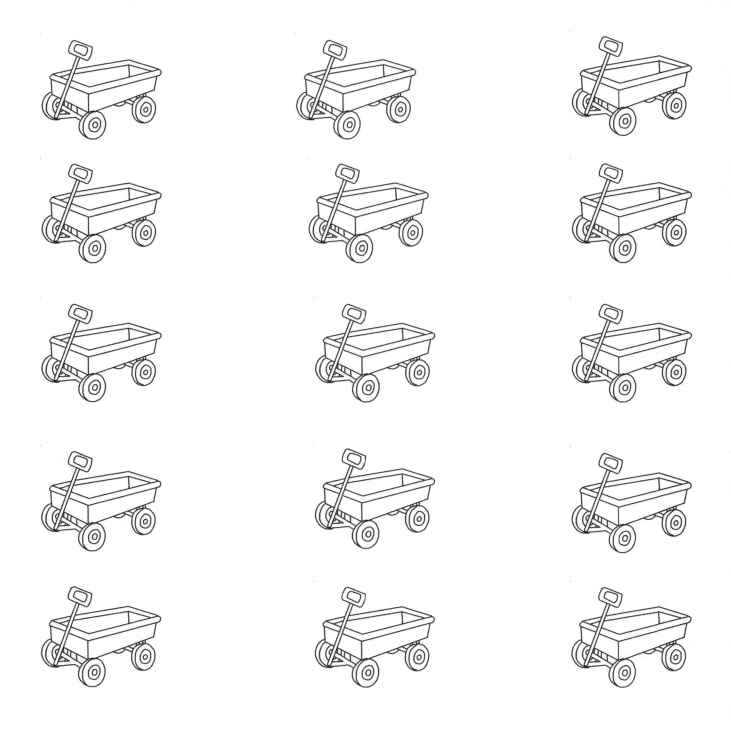

Activity #2

Create Your Own Counting Activity. Borrow a set of dice (2) and each time you roll the dice, count each dot that is on the first dice and that number goes on line 1 and then count each dot that is on the second dot and then add them up.

How many dots did you count?

Let's go!

How Many Dots?

Dice #1_____ **+ Dice #2**_____ **- How Many Total?**_____

Dice #1_____ **+ Dice #2**_____ **- How Many Total?**_____

Dice #1_____ **+ Dice #2**_____ **- How Many Total?**_____

Dice #1_____ **+ Dice #2**_____ **- How Many Total?**_____

Dice #1_____ **+ Dice #2**_____ **- How Many Total?**_____

Dice #1_____ **+ Dice #2**_____ **- How Many Total?**_____

Dice #1_____ **+ Dice #2**_____ **- How Many Total?**_____

Dice #1_____ **+ Dice #2**_____ **- How Many Total?**_____

Dice #1_____ **+ Dice #2**_____ **- How Many Total?**_____

Dice #1_____ **+ Dice #2**_____ **- How Many Total?**_____

Dice #1_____ **+ Dice #2**_____ **- How Many Total?**_____

Dice #1_____ **+ Dice #2**_____ **- How Many Total?**_____

How Many Dots?

Dice #1_____ + Dice #2_____ - How Many Total?_____

Dice #1_____ + Dice #2_____ - How Many Total?_____

Dice #1_____ + Dice #2_____ - How Many Total?_____

Dice #1_____ + Dice #2_____ - How Many Total?_____

Dice #1_____ + Dice #2_____ - How Many Total?_____

Dice #1_____ + Dice #2_____ - How Many Total?_____

Dice #1_____ + Dice #2_____ - How Many Total?_____

Dice #1_____ + Dice #2_____ - How Many Total?_____

Dice #1_____ + Dice #2_____ - How Many Total?_____

Dice #1_____ + Dice #2_____ - How Many Total?_____

Dice #1_____ + Dice #2_____ - How Many Total?_____

Dice #1_____ + Dice #2_____ - How Many Total?_____

How Many Dots?

Dice #1_____ **+ Dice #2**_____ **- How Many Total?**_____

Dice #1_____ **+ Dice #2**_____ **- How Many Total?**_____

Dice #1_____ **+ Dice #2**_____ **- How Many Total?**_____

Dice #1_____ **+ Dice #2**_____ **- How Many Total?**_____

Dice #1_____ **+ Dice #2**_____ **- How Many Total?**_____

Dice #1_____ **+ Dice #2**_____ **- How Many Total?**_____

Dice #1_____ **+ Dice #2**_____ **- How Many Total?**_____

Dice #1_____ **+ Dice #2**_____ **- How Many Total?**_____

Dice #1_____ **+ Dice #2**_____ **- How Many Total?**_____

Dice #1_____ **+ Dice #2**_____ **- How Many Total?**_____

Dice #1_____ **+ Dice #2**_____ **- How Many Total?**_____

Dice #1_____ **+ Dice #2**_____ **- How Many Total?**_____

How Many Dots?

Dice #1_____ + Dice #2_____ - How Many Total?_____

Dice #1_____ + Dice #2_____ - How Many Total?_____

Dice #1_____ + Dice #2_____ - How Many Total?_____

Dice #1_____ + Dice #2_____ - How Many Total?_____

Dice #1_____ + Dice #2_____ - How Many Total?_____

Dice #1_____ + Dice #2_____ - How Many Total?_____

Dice #1_____ + Dice #2_____ - How Many Total?_____

Dice #1_____ + Dice #2_____ - How Many Total?_____

Dice #1_____ + Dice #2_____ - How Many Total?_____

Dice #1_____ + Dice #2_____ - How Many Total?_____

Dice #1_____ + Dice #2_____ - How Many Total?_____

Dice #1_____ + Dice #2_____ - How Many Total?_____

How Many Dots?

Dice #1_____ + Dice #2_____ - How Many Total?_____

Dice #1_____ + Dice #2_____ - How Many Total?_____

Dice #1_____ + Dice #2_____ - How Many Total?_____

Dice #1_____ + Dice #2_____ - How Many Total?_____

Dice #1_____ + Dice #2_____ - How Many Total?_____

Dice #1_____ + Dice #2_____ - How Many Total?_____

Dice #1_____ + Dice #2_____ - How Many Total?_____

Dice #1_____ + Dice #2_____ - How Many Total?_____

Dice #1_____ + Dice #2_____ - How Many Total?_____

Dice #1_____ + Dice #2_____ - How Many Total?_____

Dice #1_____ + Dice #2_____ - How Many Total?_____

Dice #1_____ + Dice #2_____ - How Many Total?_____

Practice Pages

Learning numbers

1
2
3
4
5
6
7
8
9
10

Learning numbers

1
2
3
4
5
6
7
8
9
10

Learning numbers

1 1 1 1 1 1 1 1 1 1
2 2 2 2 2 2 2 2 2 2
3 3 3 3 3 3 3 3 3 3
4 4 4 4 4 4 4 4 4 4
5 5 5 5 5 5 5 5 5 5
6 6 6 6 6 6 6 6 6 6
7 7 7 7 7 7 7 7 7 7
8 8 8 8 8 8 8 8 8 8
9 9 9 9 9 9 9 9 9 9
10 10 10 10 10 10 10 10 10 10

Learning numbers

1 1 1 1 1 1 1 1 1 1 1

2 2 2 2 2 2 2 2 2 2 2

3 3 3 3 3 3 3 3 3 3 3

4 4 4 4 4 4 4 4 4 4 4

5 5 5 5 5 5 5 5 5 5 5

6 6 6 6 6 6 6 6 6 6 6

7 7 7 7 7 7 7 7 7 7 7

8 8 8 8 8 8 8 8 8 8 8

9 9 9 9 9 9 9 9 9 9 9

10 10 10 10 10 10 10 10

Learning numbers

1
2
3
4
5
6
7
8
9
10

Thank you so much for the support of my book, 1, 2, 3 Count What You See. I trust that you will utilize the activities and strategies in the book over and over as you learn your numbers, how to add them and more. For more information or to contact Julia Royston,

email me at bkroystonpublishing@gmail.com. Below are even more books by Julia Royston, and to purchase, visit www.juliaroystonstore.com.

Made in the USA
Monee, IL
31 March 2023